30 Jan 11

Stephanie,

May God continue to bless you and your family. Keep putting God first. Matt 6:33. Welcome to the family.

Shalom

MY STORMY JOURNEY

A Window to my Soul

Shalawn F. Harris

authorHOUSE®

AuthorHouse™
1663 Liberty Drive
Bloomington, IN 47403
www.authorhouse.com
Phone: 1-800-839-8640

First published by AuthorHouse   6/1/2010

ISBN: 978-1-4520-1091-5 (sc)

Library of Congress Control Number: 2010905334

Printed in the United States of America
Bloomington, Indiana

This book is printed on acid-free paper.

A Note from the Author

My stormy journey is a work that had been unwritten and unspoken for many years. Others have spoken and written of their own stormy pasts, but for many who embrace my work, this will be the first encounter of what has been hiding behind my outer shell. I always knew that I had a need and a desire to put my story on paper for others to share. I truly believe that there are so many others who will be able to relate to my journey of dealing with the loss of someone dear, struggling through the pits of depression, and trying daily to live past the emotional pain of sexual abuse as a child.

For many years I hid my feelings from my loved ones, including my own mother. Due to my mother's constant battle with drugs and alcohol during my childhood, we did not have the communication of a typical mother and daughter. We lived apart more than we lived together. Our relationship was mended during my adult years prior to her untimely death, but she remained unaware of the unfortunate abuse I suffered because I chose to keep her in the dark.

Life has its highs as well as its lows. Sometimes there were lows that I never knew I would reach. I have come to the realization that while I was at my low points there was quite a bit of learning that I needed to do. I had quite a bit of unforeseen strength and, more than anything, I had quite a bit of forgiving to do. It was during a plateau that I met a man who helped me to learn that I deserved to be at the top of every mountain everyday. It was this man who was the first to learn of my stormy journey and yet he allowed me to be myself. He has shown me highs that I had never dreamed of, mainly because I never knew that anything like this really existed. He always said I had a testimony, but I thought I was doing good just making it through another day without revisiting any of those pains. I was wrong and he was right. It is not enough just to make it through.

Throughout my journey I have learned, grown, rejoiced, and cried over and over again. I believe every one has a purpose and mine has just been unveiled. Without these storms I would not be the person I am today. There is a reason for everything and I believe that what didn't break me helped to make me that much stronger. There are many that I could blame for the troubles in my life, but rather than point blame I have chosen to overcome every stumbling block that was thrown in my way.

Many of the writings in this work are true to my personal life, but a few are true to others who have allowed me to peer through the windows of their souls for a short time.

To all those who thought I would be nothing more than a statistic, count it somewhere else. I refused to be a part of those numbers.

To all those who have been there by my side as well as behind me to help hold me up when I was down, thank you. I am making it through every day one day at a time as I continue to put my trust in the Lord (Proverbs 3:5).

To my two beautiful and precious children, mommy loves you more than you ever will know.

To my most wonderful and loving husband, thank you for showing me the unconditional love that I never knew was possible. You are my

#2 man, because as you know God always comes first, and without Him we would not have been possible. Thank you, honey, for being the king of our castle. Thank you for being my umbrella through my stormy journey. More than anything, thank you for continuing to walk beside me during our Christian Journey. I love you more and more each day.

Thank you God for everything, especially for blessing me with the wisdom to choose you and him.

Contents

Part I:The Storm   1

I'll See You After While   2
Things Won't Bring Her Back   3
It's an Anniversary   4
The Visit   5
Ghosts   6
A Doctor of the Soul   7
I am my Mother's Daughter, but she is Not me 8
You'll Never Know   10
I Rolled my Sleeves Down   11
Tears of the soul . . .   12
My Confession   13
You Don't Want to Walk in my Shoes   14
Home Base   15
Running   17
The Letter   18
Into Me   19
Is it Really Love?   20
Are You Up For The Fight?   21
Only 24   22
Will You Always?   23
Answer Me   24
This I See   25
The Single Wife   27
Something. . . To Drink   29

Part II:The Calm   **31**

Thank You	*32*
My Spiritual Journey	*33*
I Had a Lot to Learn	*34*
Thanks to my Donor	*35*
It's A Prosthetic	*36*
In Spite of. . .	*37*
The Race of my Life	*38*
Dancing In the Rain the Storm Brought In	*39*
It's Time to Rise Above It	*40*
Perfectly Imperfect	*42*
The Release	*43*
The Unveiling of Me	*44*
I'm Going For Broke	*45*
I Thought I Was All Alone	*46*
He Gave me Water, Not From the Well	*48*
Survival Road	*49*
I Am Only Human	*50*
A Love So Deep	*51*
He Loved Me Past the Pain	*52*

Part I:
The Storm

I'll See You After While

Today when I awoke
You were already gone.
"Wait for me" I thought
As my tears caused me to choke.
I didn't want to be left behind to face a day without you.
Our journey through life together was for only a short
time.
Everything is going to be okay now
because you have been set free from this world of heartache
and physical pain and sorrow.
You just keep smiling that big beautiful smile
as you continue to be my example of true strength,
kindness and courage,
and I'll see you after while.

Your one and only

Things Won't Bring Her Back

No more are the days of old
where a prayer arouses the dead.
But, a prayer doesn't hurt.
No matter how much this world provides,
It can't replace nor substitute
what I've lost forever.
With only memories that remain,
they still can't bring her back.
Waking up just before three doesn't stop time from ticking
or bring back time
that has already passed.
Tomorrow can't bring her back,
not even my yesterdays.
I only have today
that still won't bring her back.
Endless tears flowing from an aching heart
will never bring her back.
These things just won't bring her back.

It's an Anniversary

A new day arrives
With a new purpose on its horizon.
A new day, but another milestone.
Maybe another day
Not promised or foreseen.
Maybe another hour
For opportunities unknown.
Maybe another minute
To pause and acknowledge a loved one.
Maybe another second
That allowed death to pass us by.
Maybe another breath
To whisper a final goodbye.
Maybe another year
To celebrate life,
joy,
Marriage,
births,
salvation.
Maybe another year
To remember pain,
the tears,
hurt,
a loss,
a death.
None the less, it is a new day.
It's an anniversary.

The Visit

You came to visit, very unexpectedly.
You just showed up out of the blue.
You had no particular purpose
other than to make sure I'm surviving.
Your words were few
and your smile was bright.
The love in your heart
was visible in your eyes.
There was not much you had to say,
for your presence was really enough.
The time of your departure
came so abruptly
as I frantically reached over to silence the alarm.
Your spirit is always near,
even for short visits.

Ghosts

Call them shadows, call them skeletons, call them secrets,
Call them what you may.
I call them ghosts.
They are nothing more than horrible memories of the past.
Memories that bring tears to my eyes in the daylight hours,
Out of control night sweats,
And silent screams of terror during
The supposedly peaceful hours of the night.
Just when I think the ghosts have gone into hiding
And I have been released from their dominance,
They resurface just long enough to let me know
That I am in control of nothing.
Do these ghosts control me?
Maybe they have a dimunitive dominion over a miniscule
part of my life,
But it is an unyielding hold.
They want to rule over my life
And make me believe there is no hope.
They want me to give up and stop believing in me.
They want to ruin me, destroy me,
And cause me nothing but pain.
Unbeknownst to these ghosts
That they may be able to cause me misery,
Restless nights,
And emotional despair,
But they can never kill my spirit.
They are only ghosts of the past,
Trying to detour my hopes of the future.
They are only GHOSTS.

A Doctor of the Soul

I have an ache deep inside,
A burning torment that I often try to hide.
You see, I tried talking to those who said they wanted to
help;
But it was only so much that they could do.
Drugs will only numb the pangs.
I don't want numbness.
I'm tired of that feeling.
I want a total body healing.
Not just someone to tell me to pop a pill,
Or someone to tell me how to keep coping daily.
I need someone who can heal my physical,
Mental,
And spiritual being.
Someone who can make me whole.
I need a doctor of the soul.

S. F. Harris

I am my Mother's Daughter, but she is Not me

I am my mother's daughter,
but she is not me.
We have that same warm and welcoming smile.
We have that same sense of wanting to help all who hurt
and are in need.
We have that same feminine walk
that turns the head of even a visually challenged man.
We have the same sense of stubbornness
and the need to be in control.
But one day I awoke and realized
I am me, and she is she.
She abused her body
and allowed others to do the same.
She put out of her conscious
the true meaning of love.
She lost all control, hope, faith
and wanted no guidance.
She gave in to the world of darkness
and left the light.
She quickly went down,
she went under,
she went around,
but only in search of more fool's gold.
We slept silently in a false sense of security.
I awoke one day and began to see
the lessons she had to offer me.
I began to see that she would continue
to go her way, with or without me;
But I desperately needed to go my own.
My love was not strong enough
to hide the world from her,
to protect her from the world,
or even to protect her from herself.
My love was not enough.

I slept for years trying to put the affliction in a coma;
but I awoke only to a different day and time;
same agony.
I awoke one day and realized
that I am my mother's daughter,
but she is not me.

S. F. Harris

You'll Never Know

You'll never know
how much she looks like us,
how she walks with a sway,
and how she's learned to fuss.
You'll never know
how much she loves to be close
and look in your face
and tell you truthfully
what you may be feeling the most.
Even at her age
she can read my eyes
and her heart reaches out
when she can't dry her mother's endless cries.
She's so loving, but sassy.
She has your spunk,
but for you to not be here to see her
I never would have thunk.
You'll never know
the beautiful smile that you've passed to her
or how so very much
she cares for her big brother.
You'll never know
what her tender years were like,
or even what trials lay ahead
as we continue our journey in this life.
You'll never know
the tender kisses to be cherished
or the gentle, yet loving hugs
that she's learned to embellish.
You'll never know
how much she may be more like you than me.
You'll never know
that as I watch her
I'm watching your memory.

I Rolled my Sleeves Down

*I rolled my sleeves up
and put my hand to the plow
to dig deep from inside
at attempts to cover the battle scars.
I didn't want the blisters of my life
to be evident to the world.
I wanted to hide my hurt, my pain,
my secret angst of failure.
I couldn't let anyone see that I
had a softer, nicer, gentler side;
heaven forbid someone found out
I actually had feelings.
I was embarrassed to let anyone know
that I had a past,
that I was hurting,
that I had unfulfilled needs,
and more than anything
I needed to feel truly loved.
So rather than share with those
who professed their love,
I rolled my sleeves down,
hid my battle scars even deeper,
and continued on through life's journey.*

Tears of the soul . . .

. . . oh, what a story they tell . . .
Tell me a story . . .
Of where the tears come from,
Of what causes the tears to roll from deep within your soul.
Tell me a story . . .
Of the wrong that has been done,
Of how it makes you sorrowful.
Tell me a story . . .
Of what will stop the tears,
What can dry the stream,
And what will heal your soul.
Tell me a story . . .
Of how Jesus saves.
How only He can help me overcome
My strongest fears.
Tell me the story . . .
Of the tears of the soul.

My Confession

I have a confession that only a few know.
I had to hold it in to myself for so long
because I had no one else to which to go.
I debated many years on whether to let it out;
so much so that at times I just wanted to shout.
But who would believe me
and accept my gruesome honesty?
Would they call me a liar to my face
and accuse me of only trying to reach a victim's place?
Would they even be willing to listen to what I had to say?
Or would they simply dismiss me away?
Do they even want to know the whole story
of what happened behind closed doors,
and sometimes early mornings?
Could they bear to hear
how an innocence was taken
far too prematurely
to even have been given?
Would they want to know
the who,
the whens,
and how long?
Or would they rather
me just keep forging along?
Should I just try to bury
this secret back inside
and continue
to just let it hide?
If I tell you my confession,
will you keep it in your possession?
I will tell you nothing but the truth
and promise no lies.
Please forgive me
if I sometimes pause to cry.
The truth of the matter is,
this is my confession
and you will never get his.

You Don't Want to Walk in my Shoes

They always say you never can tell
what someone is going through
until you've walked a mile in their shoes.
Once you've walked the first mile,
that only gives you a brief observation of their reality.
So go ahead, walk another.
Now their world is in your view.
There is still so much not yet revealed
that remains unknown.
So go ahead, walk another.
The outer mask of wealth and happiness
is no longer all that you can envision.
The pain, the hurt, the abandonment,
the neglect, and the abuse
are making themselves known.
Go ahead, walk another.
Their paradigm is now real to you too.
You now have an idea
of what they have been carrying
through life as they walked.
Go ahead, walk another.
Tired of walking in those shoes?
So you're ready
to put yours back on?
Yours aren't so bad after all.
See, you don't want to walk in my shoes.

Home Base

This is such a familiar place to be.
A place within my comfort zone
where I can just be me.
I don't have to adjust to others,
I let others adjust to me.
Home base is not a place I like,
it's just well known.
Home base is where I go after I've given up
on what the world has to offer.
Home base is where I go
after the world has given up on me.
Home base is where I go
after I've already run the other three.
I first run to an almost equally familiar setting
of feeling the victim
and that everyone is going
to hurt me or already has;
I just may not yet know it.
After rounding the first corner
I come to the realization
that no one is really
paying any attention to me.
No one really cares
what I do, say, or think.
No one can or will
provide for me, except me.
After passing by this familiar yet lonely
location, the next stop is also a quiet spot.
No one dares to stay here with me.
They have all come
and decided to leave me here.
They have rejected my thoughts,
ideas, beliefs, attitude,
and lastly and most importantly, me.

They despise my beauty,
my confidence,
and my desires to be more.
But there's no place like home.
There's no place more familiar
than that feeling of knowing
that you're going to be left.
Don't know when
and not always sure why,
but none the less
the time will certainly come.
I'm tired of always being left behind,
being rejected, neglected, and abused.
I'll stay in constant watch
for the day I shall finally land
at my home base
and choose to leave you
before you leave me.
The familiar and guarded place
of my home base
that leads me to believe
that I'll always be
the one left behind.
It's my home base.
It's home.
It's safe.

Running

My feet grow weary from the exorbitant
amount of traffic I've caused my soles.
I've left the only home I've ever known;
uncertain of where my journey leads me.
I've tried to leave the ghosts, rumors,
skeletons, and nightmares behind.
They keep following me and I just keep running.
I've tried to erase the memories
and even parts of the past,
but it's just not in my power to do.
So I just keep running.
A momentary pause for an instantaneous glance
at reality is so unbearable
I can't catch my breath.
So I just keep running.
I can't look back
because it knows my face
and will find it easier
to dissipate the lead I've gained.
I just keep running.
Sometimes I run in circles,
but usually just from base to base.
When will I break the cycle
of taking on the roles
of victim, abused, neglected, rejected, orphaned?
When will I finally deal with what I'm running from
so that one day I can reveal
who I really am,
discard my threadbare shoes,
rest my exasperated soul,
and stop running?
I don't know,
and neither does anyone else.
Until then,
I'll just keep running.

The Letter

I sent a letter some time ago;
how long I just don't know.
It was sent to a love from times past.
Not a love with any type of sexual involvement,
but a lovely friendship that didn't last.
I professed my many imperfections
and how life had changed how I viewed
all of my present, past and future relations.
As a witness to how foolish youth can be,
I pleaded for forgiveness and asked for
an opportunity to see a new me.
I expressed how through death
I've learned to live again
and to challenge life for a win.
I tried to petition my case
as I continued to write
with tears streaming down my face.
I poured out my heart,
thinking that I had done my part.
I waited for a response to come,
positive or negative.
Not a one.
Maybe it went undelivered
and my words unread;
none the less, I can't get it out of my head.
Maybe no response is your answer.
Unfortunately, it is one that I can not hear.

Into Me

Can you know what my name is,
more than just my first?
Can you tell me the color
that's peeping back at you?
Hazel, gray, blue.
Which is my favorite?
Red, purple, black, green.
Do you know anyone in my family tree?
Do you know what makes me shout for joy?
Do I like long walks, explicit talks,
a good book, or only how I look?
Am I concerned about what you can do for me,
promise me, or buy me?
Do I care if you may drive a whip,
make less than me, or that you might
ride the bus?
Can you describe the look on my face
when I'm totally fed up
and all hell is about to break loose?
Can you tell me what pushes my buttons
and drives me over the edge?
Do you care how sometimes
I feel like everyone in the world
is up when I feel down?
Do you care that sometimes
I may have love for you
and at the same time
not want to be around you?
Can you see how immature you can be
by not first getting to know me?
Do you even comprehend
how enjoyable all of me can be?
So before you try to get in to me,
can you try to get into me?

Is it Really Love?

They say love is blind,
but it was love at first sight.
They say love is forever,
but you left when things got hard.
They say love is pure,
but you corrupted it when you let others
divide our oneness.
They say love is patient,
but you wouldn't wait
on me until we said "I do."
They say love is not conceited,
but it's always you first and not me.
They say love rejoices in the truth,
but time after time
you fed me lie after lie.
They say love endures all things,
but you had to take
a temporary leave
when I had a temporary downfall.
They say love is sometimes a crazy,
wild, out of control whirlwind
that can catch you up all of a sudden.
Love can be whatever
we want it to be
for that particular
time, place, and person.
Is it really love
or am I just that stupid?

Are You Up For The Fight?

We're together in name and deed,
but are we spiritually?
We were warned of things to come
that will break up our home.
Everyone on the outside looking in
see fake smiles, fronts, and a sense of impending doom.
The house is beautiful,
but why can't we make it a home?
The account is open,
but does it have to be shared with all?
Can we get together
and practice
pleasing one another
like we once did?
The distractions in front of us
are money, lust, and outside family.
We keep coming back to this point
because we fail to solve the problem.
We keep talking,
but I'm not hearing you
and apparently
you're not hearing me.
We keep saying we're going to stay together
and move on through
these trying times.
We keep saying we're not going
to allow the devil to divide us,
but we keep inviting him into our home
as if he has the answers we need.
You want to stay together,
but are you up for the fight?

S. F. Harris

Only 24

The day seems so long
when things are going wrong.
The day seems so short
when all is of a great sort.
So many things to be done in a day's time.
After it's completion, a simple line.
The schedule is overflowing
with work, kids, and good deeds,
but no time just for blowing.
I would like to sit and watch TV all day,
or even sit and watch the kids play.
I would like to sleep until my body gets sore,
but somebody has got to go to the grocery store.
I would even like to sit and read a book
all the way through,
but there are so many other things to do.
I have made a list of things to be done,
but that's all under today's sun.
With a new day brings new chores
and I never know what interruptions
lay in store.
If I take a short break
that might be a mistake.
With so many things left to do
I may never get through.
One day rolls into another
with the need to complete the task
of a different day's deeds.
I know. I know. I'm not alone
and nor do I sorrow.
I only have 24 hours,
like everyone else,
with none on loan
and none to borrow.

Will You Always?

You said you loved me
and that you would
do anything for me.
Will you always?
You said the world was mine
and all I had to do was ask
and you would get it.
Will you always?
You made a promise to love
only me
and forsake all others.
Will you always?
You said you would always
be here for our family
and only put God before us.
Will you always?
You said you would forgive
even the most
unforgivable.
Will you always?
You said "I do"
before God
and family.
Will you always?

Answer Me

What was that you said?
Did I not hear you correctly?
Are you asking me or telling me?
Is that a demand?
Have you no respect for me or yourself?
You want me to do what?
Are you that insane?
Do you not care about me or yourself?
How do you live with yourself?
How can you look at your reflection in the mirror?
Do you not have any feelings?
Are you even human?
Do you not have any remorse?
Do you not feel any shame?
Do you not feel any guilt for your actions that have hurt so
many?
Can you look me in my eyes and answer me?

This I See

You stole my heart away
and promised to care for it day after day
but now I see.
You said 'I love you'
that you 'would never leave'
or find another like me,
but now I see.
You said 'Don't leave me'
and that you would "change'
because you wanted me to be happy,
but now I see.
Day by day my eyes open wider and brighter
to allow me to now see.
I see that as the sun rises,
so it sets daily.
This I do now see.
I see that as a rose blooms,
so does it eventually die.
This I do now see.
I see that as the moon appears in the night,
so does it daily disappear.
This I do now see.
I see that as feelings come,
so do they also melt away.
This I do now see.
I see that as some people change,
so do some people remain the same.
This I do now see.
Just as I saw the sun,
I saw us as one.
Just as I saw the tides roll in,
I saw us fall apart.
Just as I saw the rose bloom,
I saw us growing further apart.

S. F. Harris

Just as I saw the moon disappear,
I saw you fading away.
Just as I saw my feelings come,
I saw my feelings melt away.
Just as I saw myself change,
I saw you remain the same.
My eyes are open
and I do now see.

The Single Wife

The vows were beautiful
and so was the day.
You promised your life and love
until our last days.
There was no guarantee
for a life without difficulty
nor was there a false promise
of sharing in the laundry.
We both work hard
outside of the home
trying to raise our kids
and be successful on our own.
For the most part
all is well;
but some times
I feel like I'm in a living hell.
You're here at times
"spending time with the family"
but mostly only here in the flesh,
while I run around playing mommy and daddy.
Most times you do as expected
and you are very helpful,
but sometimes your eyes are blinded
to the household chores.
Sometimes it's as if you don't even see
that there are things to be done
to take care of the house
and not really much time for fun.
I would love to chill out
and kick up my feet
and enjoy some quiet time
when I'm feeling tired and beat.

S. F. Harris

And yet the day goes on
winding down quickly
as I run out of time;
for my things to do list is lengthy.
The list could be shortened,
even taken off of my hands
every once in a while,
but that thought is too grand.
Yes, I know.
I signed up for this flight,
but no one ever told me
of the frustration that blurs my sight.
I said yes to marriage
and being your wife.
I thought that I was
leaving behind the single life.
I'm not alone,
but just the same;
the chores are all mine
as well as the kids who keep calling my name.
They know who you are
and they know what you sometimes do,
but even outsiders
know these things too.
Help me to understand
how things turned around,
because I can't quite recall
how it is that there's so much free time
that you have somehow found.
You always have time
to chat and mingle,
but can you explain to me
why I am married, but feel so single?

Something. . . To Drink

I was out there for quite some time.
I tasted and was tasted by some of the best.
A few only needed a drink for that day
and quickly discarded anything remaining.
A few needed a drink to get them through their desert,
but when the drought was over
I still had a thirst of my own.
Some drank but never offered to pour,
leaving me empty and parched.
My search for that perfect drink
was becoming a distant mirage.
I became down right thirsty
and no ordinary drink was going to do.
I was in need of something strong, not weak;
something stiff, not fruity;
something lasting, not temporary;
something hard, not soft;
something. . .something.
Something.
Something that could satisfy my most insatiable thirst
and make me want to become sober
and never pick up another.
I need something. . .to drink.

Part II:
The Calm

Thank You

Thank you for all that you do,
both great and small.
Thank you for being you,
ruler of all.
Thank you for the joys,
as well as the pains,
and all of the triumphant gains.
Thank you for the sense of security that you give,
as I try to survive
this wicked world in which I live.
Thank you for holding on to me,
even when I didn't know
I needed to be held.
I just thought I needed to be free.
Thank you for keeping me close
to your heart,
even when my own heart
had been repeatedly torn apart.
Thank you for not
passing me by on the side of the road
as others went on their way,
because too heavy was my load.
Thank you for dusting me off
after my numerous falls,
and granting me your grace and mercy
to keep my head up
through it all.

My Spiritual Journey

We all have a time or place that we first began our journey.
There was a person or a place that changed our whole lives.
Someone who knew that we were headed for a dead end,
Or even a life of nothing but self-destruction.
They helped plant the seeds of life that didn't convince us all at once,
But made us think of how we wanted to spend eternity.
Destruction on earth with continued destruction forever after,
Or do I choose Christ and look forward to eternal bliss?
The timing was right for the seeds to grow.
This hell on earth made anything worth trying.
Just one walk down the spiritual path seemed to open up a whole new perspective of the world.
As I journeyed further, I realized that this was not only worth trying,
But something worth dying for.
This spiritual journey has taken me places that I never even thought possible.
I have gained the faith that it takes to believe that I can accomplish the impossible.
Only through this spiritual journey have I learned to love and be loved,
Forgive and be forgiven,
Trust and be trusted,
Believe and allow Him to be believed through me.

I Had a Lot to Learn

I knew how to play the game of catch,
but I didn't know how to play for keeps.
I knew how to be a freak,
but I didn't know how to be the lady
you also needed me to be.
I knew how to touch you
and make you feel special,
but I didn't know how to hold you
and make you feel loved.
I knew how to tell you
what you wanted to hear,
but I didn't know how
to tell you what I needed most.
I knew how to
take care of myself,
but I didn't know how
to take care of the needs of others.
I knew how a loving family
was supposed to be,
but I didn't know
that I was meant to be a part of that family.
I knew what love was supposed to be,
but I didn't know
how to be loved.
I knew that you loved me,
but I just didn't know how to love me.
I knew that you would
still love me,
but I had to learn
how to truly love you back.

Thanks to my Donor

Thank you for your contribution
of all that you had to pass on.
Thank you for your contribution
of more than you could ever imagine.
Thank you for all those
large and small parts that
helped to make me.
Thanks goes to my donor
for his contribution of his DNA.
Basically that's all he bothered to give;
and surprisingly,
that was more than enough for me.
So, thanks to my donor.

S. F. Harris

It's A Prosthetic

I had to get rid of it.
It was getting in the way.
Always getting soft, never staying strong;
not able to withstand tough times,
just giving out when the roughest storms came.
It would serve its purpose occasionally;
after all, I'm still alive.
But it often lead me off course
to not following what was a better source.
I just had to have it cut out
because I would rather do without.
Now nothing can soften or weaken my heart
because it's a prosthetic,
and that may be the best part.

In Spite of. . .

In spite of the often tough times
and the numerous bad times
that outweighed the good,
I succeeded.
In spite of sometimes going hungry
to feed the little ones
who could not comprehend
the plight of their torture,
I succeeded.
In spite of occasionally stealing money
from the mysterious visitors
that transgressed,
I succeeded.
In spite of blatantly lying
and telling others I was an orphan
because I often felt just that alone,
I succeeded.
In spite of the numerous
tough times,
the unfulfilled promises,
the heart-wrenching let downs,
the multiple mistakes,
and the soul-stirring trauma,
there have been some rays of sun.
In spite of it all,
the sun continued to shine on me
when the rain fell no more.
In spite of. . .

The Race of my Life

The decision was made to compete;
not for a prize, for recognition, or gain.
The training became a way to escape
from the depressing thoughts, the financial worries,
job stressors, flimsy friends, treacherous enemies,
ethical dilemmas, and irrefutable demons.
They all faded away with each stride.
The pain would surge out of my open pores.
No time to think, worry, contemplate, or lament;
only concentration on the next breath to come,
the next step to make,
to put me closer toward my goal.
Just breathe. . .
Clear the thoughts of doubt.
Believe in yourself and your abilities.
Just breathe. . .
Race day has come
and the sound of the starter gun
echoes in the morning air.
Thousands, maybe even tens of thousands,
of footsteps and cheers begin.
Now the fullness of life
has also come to my realization.
Here I am alone and
about to run the race of my life
in memorandum
of a life that is now only a precious thought;
and depending only
on the one who gives life.
Just breathe. . .

Dancing In the Rain the Storm Brought In

The journey has been stormy,
often dark and dreary.
Usually when the storm clouds come upon me,
I feel as if there is nothing that I can do.
Hopelessness fills my spirit
and gloom besets me.
Occasionally, when the storm clouds come
the sun will also remain.
It is those few times when my hope
remains and joy fills my spirit
because I can go out into the storm
and joyously dance in the rain
the storm brought in.
No need to feel down and out.
No need to go into hiding.
Withstand the storm before you
and around you.
While waiting for the storm to pass
just have a little dance
in the rain the storm brought in.
No specific rhythm or audible tune,
just a spirit-filled jig
that can not be controlled.
So let the sun shine during the storm
that I may dance in the rain
that the storm brought in.

S. F. Harris

It's Time to Rise Above It

A woman once told me
of the hard-knock life of another.
In her youth she had been abused,
misused and very confused.
She lacked trust in others and mostly
no confidence in herself.
Her life now consists of choice after choice
of downward, degrading, and
dead end decisions.
She merely exists to supply her next need
and to satisfy the sinful needs of others.
But now her decisions effect another.
Another who has no say, no choice, no wish,
no knowledge, not even a care, and maybe not even a
chance.
Her choices and decisions have not changed,
not even out of concern for her unborn.
She has a life-long plague
that will never leave her;
and it is possible that her unborn
may suffer that plague as well.
As I listen to this real-life drama
that happens more and more everyday,
my heart fills with disappointment, disbelief, and disdain.
The woman reads the expression on my face
and tells me that I have no right to feel the way I feel
about someone who has been dealt
such a cruel hand in life.
She doesn't know me.
She doesn't know my struggles.
She doesn't know what hand I was dealt.
I simply tell her that
things of the past
are just that.

They can be used as excuses
for not wanting to try;
crutches to signal to the world
the helpless state we feel;
bricks to build up yet another wall against others;
windows to escape from reality;
or mirrors to reflect inward,
see our own strength
and vow to never again
be defeated, abused, neglected, used,
or taken for granted.
It's time to rise up
against the excuses of the past.
It's time to rise up and face the future.

Perfectly Imperfect

Each one of us He breathed His breath into us.
He gave us the strength to move and to support our own
beings.
He gave us the ability to think and choose for ourselves.
Each one of us is the same, yet different.
A mole here, a tag there;
A dimple up here, a stretch mark over there;
A bushy do, a lonely strand;
A sun-kissed bronze, a tasty caramel;
A dove's likeness, a milk chocolate bar;
The arthritic knee, the pulled hamstring;
The tennis elbow, the carpel tunnel wrist;
The over-expanded waistline, the wash board abs;
The bulging biceps, the turkey wing triceps;
The apple bottom, the trunk too full of junk;
The muscle carved calves, the cankles.
Each one of us share one of these likenesses
because we are all
perfectly imperfect.

The Release

I've held on for so long
to the pain, the abuse, the neglect,
and emotional burdens.
I've held them so tight
my knuckles are white
and my flesh drips crimson.
I've held on for so long
that I never looked around
to see anyone
willing to give me a break
and hold on a moment for me.
I've held on for so long
that I wouldn't even know
what it would be like
to relax the muscles
of my digits and limbs
and to open up my hand
and just let go.
I've held on for so long
that to let go might mean
that I would have to be vulnerable
to someone who might want
to pick up my burden.
I've held on for so long
that to let go might mean
that both my body and mind
might be able to receive
the rest they undoubtedly deserve.
I've held on for so long
that I subconsciously feel
that to let go would mean
a loss of control, power, even sanity.
I've held on for so long
that I just can't do it any longer.
I must finally take a deep breath
and just simply
release.

The Unveiling of Me

Please don't stare
don't say a word.
I want you to notice,
but I don't want you to have
such a look of bewilderment.
I'll show you my wounds,
some are still bare, yet old.
Others are well-healed,
but the scabs
are feeble.
I know. I know.
They're a horrible sight to bear.
I want you to really see
what's been brewing
inside for so long.
Behold the scars
that try to cover
my inner beauty
as I begin
the unveiling of me.

I'm Going For Broke

I have no more purchasing power.
I have nothing to lend.
An unbelievable deal came along
and I just couldn't pass it up.
I took into consideration the time
I may have left
and what temptation
I may have to pass up.
My thoughts were only
on what was before me,
what I would be leaving behind,
and what I had to look forward to.
I've emptied my pockets,
my purse, my heart, and my soul
just for this one
perfect opportunity.
I sold out to the Lord.
I gave Him my everything, my all.
No more perpetrating the life,
but instead actually living the talk.
No more trusting in others
who I can depend on to let me down.
I'm putting my everything in Him
and I'm going for broke.

S. F. Harris

I Thought I Was All Alone

The way seemed so dark,
the task so hard to complete.
I often felt like
I was destined to lose
and be lost forever
in this world of darkness.
So often I wanted to throw in the towel
and lay down and quit.
There were so many roadblocks
and naysayers along the way
that it was hard to hear
the small whisper coming from a place unknown.
I hesitantly trudged on
with many days of numbness
and just going through the motions.
Some days I can't recall
and others I would do anything
just to be able to forget.
I never knew that during those somber days
and sleepless nights
I was being watched.
Not only was I being watched,
but I was picked up,
brushed off, and carried out of the bottomless pit
that I had little by little
found my way into.
I struggled with the
brightness of the distinct visions before me.
I could hardly believe the unique opportunities
that were placed before me.
I did not understand how I had come
to this new place,
nor could I fathom why
I was given this second chance
at a novel beginning,

down an unfamiliar path.
I realized that it was not I
that found this place,
but that there was always
someone guiding me.
A miniscule light that kept shining through
the darkness and
a quiet still voice
that kept directing me
to its preferred path.
I thought it was my judgment,
my street savvy,
my wisdom,
or just good luck.
It was never just me,
or even you.
It has always been Him right there,
even when I thought
I was all alone.

S. F. Harris

He Gave me Water, Not From the Well

*I needed a drink
because my soul was thirsty.
He gave me water,
not from the well.
I needed something
to renew my spirit.
He gave me water,
not from the well.
I needed something
to revive my body.
He gave me water,
not from the well.
I needed something
to refill my joy.
He gave me water,
not from the well.
I needed something
to cleanse my mind.
He gave me water,
not from the well.
I needed something
to adjust my focus.
He gave me water,
not from the well.
I needed something
to change my life.
He gave me water,
not from the well.
I needed something
to save my soul.
He gave me water,
not from the well.*

Survival Road

I needed to find a better way
that would lead me to a different road.
The road I had already trod
had left me carrying a heavy load.
I needed to leave the scenic route
that had over exposed my tender mind.
I wanted to take the road less traveled
and leave all that mess behind.
I desired a different future
than what I had grown accustomed to.
A life of drugs, alcohol, and multiple fathers
for my children was not what I wanted to do.
I wanted to be able to have options
and exercise available opportunities.
I didn't want to have to depend on others
who were fickle and offered no guarantees.
I searched the plans of others
for solutions to how they achieved.
I had to do what successful people did
and it didn't matter what anyone else believed.
It was belief in myself and determination
to overcome the unfortunate cards
that were told to be mine.
With only success in my plans,
I turned onto survival road
leaving only a trail of tears behind.

I Am Only Human

Don't hold me too high,
for I might fall
from the pedestal you put me on.
I am only human after all.
Don't hold me in too high regard
for I might fall
from your graces.
I am only human after all.
Don't think me beyond
the ability to fall prey to sins
that overtake all.
I am only human after all.
Don't think me too good
to have a problem
that may be big or small.
I am only human after all.
Don't think me too special
to make a call
in the need of prayer.
I am only human after all.
Don't think me incapable
of occasionally hitting a wall
because things get too tough.
I am only human after all.
Don't hold me too high
because I just might fall
from the pedestal you put me on.
I am only human after all.

A Love So Deep

It warms you to the core.
It makes your hairs stand on end.
It gives you a queasy feeling in the pit of your stomach.
It gives you a light-headed feeling with the simple thought.
It makes your lips quiver for a long-awaited kiss.
It makes your heart beat to its own irregular rhythm.
It makes your breast rise to the occasion.
It makes you cross your legs just to control the pulsations
of your loins.
It makes your toes curl with the slightest embrace.
It takes your breath away when he whispers your name.
It brings tears to your eyes when you reach the top
together.
It makes you arch your back with the slightest thought
that there will be more to follow.
It makes your head swim with the thoughts of your recent
events.
It makes you want to give your all-in-all just to keep things
from changing.
It makes you feel like life is finally worth living.
It makes you forget the pain of the past.
It makes you look forward to the future.
A future filled with faith, hope, and love.
Have you ever had a love so deep?

He Loved Me Past the Pain

He stayed by my side
even when I pushed him away;
and he never left
even when I asked him not to stay.
I was damaged goods
and felt I would only cause him pain
and heartbreak
and mountains of mental strain.
I didn't want to hurt him
so I wanted him to be free
from my living nightmare
and not one day resent me.
He tolerated the short tempers,
the highs, the lows, the mood swings,
and he even dealt with the moment
I was willing to give back his ring.
He prayed with me,
for me, and over me
trying to rid me of the torment
that I struggled with inside of me.
He said he had a heart
big enough for us two
and that he could love me
past the pain
if I allowed him to.

LaVergne, TN USA
24 July 2010
190683LV00002B/1/P